The Mighty Stallion

and other Poems

by

C. G. Ferrel

ISBN 0-9729684-1-5

Library of Congress Control Number: 2004111804

Quantity discounts are available on bulk purchases of this book for educational purposes, fundraising, etc. For details write to Acheulean Publishing, P.O. Box 6166, Rock Island, IL 61204. Please include phone number and name of contact person.

Reference Books

1. Personalities of America - Sixth Edition —
   Published by ABI (The American Biographical
   Institute).
2. International Directory of Distinguished
   Leadership - Fourth Edition — Published by
   ABI.
3. Who's Who in Poetry — Published by World of
   Poetry.
4. Who's Who in Poetry and Poet's Encyclopedia -
   Seventh Edition — Published by International
   Biographical Centre.

Publishing Credits - Poetry Anthologies
(contributor)

1. These Too Shall Be Heard Vol. I — Published by SA-DE Publications, Sam L. Vulgaris (Publisher), 1989.
2. These Too Shall Be Heard Vol. II — Published by SA-DE Publications, Sam L. Vulgaris (Publisher), 1989.
3. Golden Voices - Past and Present — Published by Fine Arts Press, Lincoln B. Young (Publisher), 1989.
4. 1990 Anthology of Southern Poetry — Published by Chuck Kramer, Great Lakes Poetry Press, Chuck Kramer (Publisher), 1990.
5. Whispers in the Wind Vol. III — Published by Quill Books, Shirley Mikkelson (Publisher), 1990.
6. American Poetry Anthology Vol. IX, No. 4 — Published by American Poetry Association, Robert Nelson (Publisher), 1990.
7. Down Peaceful Paths — Published by Quill Books, Shirley Mikkelson (Publisher), 1990.
8. Moments of Memories — Published by Publishers Press, 1990.
9. These Too Shall Be Heard Vol. III — Published by SA-DE Publications, Sam L. Vulgaris (Publisher), 1991.
10. American Poetry Anthology Vol. X, No. 2 — Published by American Poetry Association, Robert Nelson (Publisher), 1990.

11. Word Magic--A Panorama of Poetry — Published by Fine Arts Press, Lincoln B. Young (Publisher), 1991.
12. World of Poetry Anthology — Published by World of Poetry Press, John Cambell (Editor & Publisher), 1991.
13. Our World's Most Treasured Poems — Published by World of Poetry Press, John Cambell (Editor & Publisher), 1991.
14. Our World's Favorite Gold & Silver Poems — Published by World of Poetry Press, John Cambell (Editor & Publisher), 1991.
15. Poems That Will Last Forever — Published by World of Poetry Press, John Cambell (Editor & Publisher), 1991.
16. Great Poems of Our Time — Published by World of Poetry Press, John Cambell (Editor & Publisher), 1991.
17. Listen With Your Heart — Published by Quill Books, 1992.
18. These Too Shall Be Heard, Vol. IV — Published by SA-DE Publications
19. The Other Side of the Mirror — Published by Watermark Press, 1992.
20. In A Different Light — Published by The National Library of Poetry, 1992.
21. Our World's Most Favorite Poems — Published by World of Poetry, 1991.
22. A Question of Balance — Published by The National Library of Poetry, 1992.
23. Dance on the Horizon — Published by National Library of Poetry
24. At Days End — National Library of Poetry

Books

1. Think
2. The Mighty Stallion - and other Poems

Biographical Data

Name: Carl G. Ferrel

Born: Iowa City, Iowa — July 29, 1950

Marital Status: Single

Education: Degree in Culinary Art - 1973; Studied Real Estate, Economics, Business Law and Communications - 1981, Black Hawk College.

Occupation(s): Chef, Meat Cutter, Business Consultant, President (record company), Restaurant Manager, Septic Surgeon. Also Real Estate Investor and Member of Laborers Union Local #309, Rock Island, Illinois.

Memberships have included:
- Florida State Poets Association, Inc.
- National Federation of State Poetry Societies, Inc.
- National Arbor Day Foundation
- Niabi Zoological Society
- National Parks & Conservation Association
- National & International Wildlife Federation
- World Wildlife Fund
- The National Audubon Society
- Associate Member of The American Museum of Natural History
- Associate Member of The Smithsonian Associates
- Associate Member of The Illinois Sheriffs' Association
- Associate Member of The Nature Conservancy

Awards:
- Golden Poet - 1990 & 1991
- Honorable Mentions (7)
- Distinguished Leadership - 1991
- Editors Choice Award - 1996

Statement (Common Themes and Comments): I write about a variety of subjects; love, friendship, family, nature, social issues, etc. I would like to see world peace, and an end to world hunger, and the formation of an international coalition to protect and preserve the earth and its inhabitants and strive for an ecological balance between man and nature that will allow both to survive and prosper. I would also like to see a return to traditional family values.

My Advice: Seek the truth in all things. Be honest, fair, and sincere.

For additional information see:
> Bern Porter Collection of Contemporary Letters
> Miller Library, Special Collections
> Colby College
> Waterville, Maine 04901

Table of Contents

Triangle Thin

In torment I fight,
A triangle thin.
A battle in which
All must win—
Or lose—
Whichever the case may be.

I search for answers,
I cannot see.
One loves me,
Whom I love not.
The one I love
In the middle is caught.

So what do I do,
In this triangle thin,
To let everyone
In this battle win
The kind of life
They do deserve—
Filled with happiness,
Without reserve.

Life

The breath of life,
Ever so sweet.
Trees and flowers,
Ever so neat.

The river's
Never-ending flow.
The sun's
Life-giving glow.

Just look around,
What do you see?
Open the book—
There is you,
There is me—
An unwritten page
In history.

How did it start?
How shall it end?
It began with love,
But will end with sin!

For My Love

All the stars
In the sky,
For her
I shall buy.

Then,
A thousand reasons
I shall tell her
Why.

Why
I love her
So
Very much.

Why
I long for
Her tender,
Loving touch.

I shall buy for her
A castle,
Free
From strife and hassle.

Then,
I shall build a rainbow
High
Up in the sky.

Then,
I shall love her
Until
The day I die!

The Odd Couple

One
Has vivacity.
The other,
Audacity.

One is filled
With love and caring.
The other speaks
With boldness and daring.

Quite the couple
I would say.
Yes,
Quite the pair.

Yet their love
Is warm, sincere.
It keeps them
To each other near.

All in a Picture

There is a picture
On the wall
Of the country
In the fall.

Golden brown
Are the falling leaves,
A soft wind
Whispering through the trees.

It tells the tale
Of summer's end,
Hinting of a winter
Soon to begin.

Squirrels
Gathering nuts
For their nests
High up in the trees.

Birds
Drifting south
With the cool
Autumn breeze.

All I see
Is amazingly true.
The sun shines gold—
The sky, a velvet blue.

All this
Hangs in the hall,
In a picture
On the wall.

Love Is

Love is
When a quick good-bye kiss
Is not enough.

Love is
When the steak tastes tender
Even if it's tough.

Love is
Wanting to be
With her alone.

Love is
The good feeling
Of coming home.

Love is
Being with your family,
Whether it is Wednesday, Friday, or Sunday.

Together as One

Outside,
The sun is as hot
As coals in a fire.

Inside,
My heart is warm
With love
And desire.

I am filled
With a burning passion,
Though my love may seem
A bit old-fashioned.

To me it is a love
Of the finest kind.
The kind of love
So hard to find.

When
Two people alone,
Together
Are one.

And through life
With joy,
Together
They run.

And
In the autumn of life,
They share
The setting sun.

When
Two people alone,
Together
Are one.

October 17, 1975

This Friday morn,
A child was born.
On this day,
My heart was torn.

This child
Did not live
Long enough
For life to give.

Even the simplest
Little joys
A babe enjoys
From little toys.

No, for God has come
And taken away
This child with him,
Always to stay.

Yes, you may rest,
My precious child,
For the winds in heaven,
Blow ever so mild!

Bride to Be

The lovely girl
By my side,
Someday will be
My blushing bride.

We'll talk, laugh
And sometimes cry,
But our love
Will never die.

June

Love is blooming
Everywhere.
Happiness and joy
Fill the air.
Young love,
The song of spring.
A thorny rose,
A warning tune.
Wedding bells.
It's June.
It's June!

Living Is Dying

Let not
A quarrel be,
For a dying man
In ecstasy.

For if a man
Is not alive,
How can he
Truly survive.

You search for this,
And then find that.
You reach for more,
But are handed less.

You struggle in darkness,
Searching for light.
Living is dying,
And dying is life.

My Precious Angel

Like an angel
She came to me.
This lovely goddess
Set me free.

Free to live, laugh,
And love again.
To live with honor
Instead of sin.

Too wonderful for words
That I could say.
And by her side
I will always stay.

Changing Seasons

As I sit in my easy chair,
Out a window I do stare.
Yes, as I sit in my living room,
I see a lonely rose in bloom.
The grass is growing nice and neat,
Creating a green cushion for my feet.
The leaves are stirring in the wind,
Telling of autumn around the bend.
As the end of summer does draw near
Singing birds, I do still hear.
To the falling leaves they do call
As summer soon turns into fall.

Christmas Cheer

I drink a toast
Of Christmas cheer.
I drink rum,
They drink beer.

With New Year's Eve
So very near,
I wonder what
May come next year.

We drink, we laugh,
We joke and sing.
Too happy to care
About a thing.

Love Story

This is a story
Of a love so true.

This is a story
Of a heaven blue.

I have come to love
A girl so fair.

With soft brown eyes
And dark brown hair.

Much more than this,
I cannot say.

My love grows stronger
Day by day.

Her gentle eyes,
Her smile so warm.

She is my light
In any storm.

Linda

Gentle
As a turtle dove,
My precious angel
Full of love.

She is the one
That I adore,
Perfect as
The girl next door.

She makes my world
Ever so bright.
She turns the darkness
Into light.

She is my night.
She is my day.
She makes my troubles
Seem far away.

She is the one
That I love,
An angel sent
From above.

Death Reigns Supreme

Death reigns supreme
In the mighty tropical jungle
For all who live
Or dare to go there.

The fight for life—
Always the hardest fought—
Is, in the end,
The one that is always lost!

The Coming Snow

Crystals form upon the grass
Before the early morning sun.
The robin sings and spins his tale
Of winter soon to come.
Squirrels scurry on the ground
To gather nuts before the snow.
The bear fills his belly
Before his winter sleep.
The leaves quietly drift
To the ground below.
And then, like every other year,
The sky lays down a blanket
Of gently falling snow.

Long Live the King

The king
Lies in slumber
In the silence
Of his tomb.

All his worldly
Treasures
Surround him
In this room.

All his loyal
Subjects
In silence
Mourn his passing.

Do Not Wait

The secret to eternal life
Is the planting of the seed
That results in procreation.
For all who live eternally,
Do so in name and memory
Of the children they have borne
And deeds that they have done.
So, go now and procreate.
Do goodness when you can.
Do not wait til it is too late.
One never knows
When his time
Is close at hand.

Man of Destiny

Tragedy marks
A man of all seasons.
Struggle and strife—
These are the reasons.

Man's destiny
Makes the decision.
It gives him strength,
Courage, and vision.

Ever present,
There
Is an air
Of mystery

About the man
Who makes his
Place
In history.

Drip, Tick

Drip, drip, drip,
So slowly falls the blood
Of the man whose wound is fatal.

Tick, tick, tick,
So swiftly time runs out
As he tries to cling to life.

So soon
His life is over,
As he draws his final breath.

Tomorrow he will be buried.
Day after that,
He will be forgot.

The Mighty Stallion

Hooves pounding, nostrils flaring,
The stallion leads the herd,
Fleeing would-be captors
In the early morning light.
With riders flanking left and right,
Pursuit is hard and fast.
With heaving chest and pounding heart,
He races for his freedom.
But all of this, to no avail;
A canyon has him boxed.
Quickly, riders seal the gap,
Blocking all escape.
With all his might and fury
He tries to break away.
He charges at the riders,
But all of this for naught.
Because in the end,
Sad, but true,
The mighty stallion has been caught!

Ambush

A snapping twig betrays
A stranger in the night.
Hidden in the bushes,
Safely out of sight.

Now suddenly, his presence known,
His chances for
Surprise attack,
Just as quickly gone.

The waiting
Now is over.
It is time
To stand and fight.

For life,
The prize is victory.
For death,
The battle is lost!

Last Cigarette

A cigarette
Slowly burns
In an ashtray
Full of butts.

The smoker
Looks relaxed
In
His easy chair.

He wears a mask
Of peaceful slumber.
But in truth, the smoker
Really is quite dead!

Desert Run

Slowly as I walk
Across the desert sand,
Vaguely I remember
The reason that I ran,
In haste and desperation
To this barren land.
I robbed a store,
Killed a man,
And now am on the run.
In the end the law will catch me.
Then I will pay the price,
Unless the desert gets me first.
No matter what the outcome,
This run will be my last.

Life Race

Swiftly
I am running.
Then
I am slowing down.

Then
No longer can I run.
Now
I have to walk.

Then
I begin to stagger
And stumble
As I walk.

Slowly
I am falling.
Now
I have to crawl.

Now
I can no longer move.
I
Am out of breath!

Man from the Alamo

One man left the Alamo,
Supposedly of fright.
Few men knew the reason
He did not stay and fight.
Now those men who knew the truth
No longer are alive
To tell about the families
He felt he had to save.
Though, with sadness and misfortune,
He found he was too late.
The families had been murdered
By rebels of the state.

Once the Die Is Cast

So hard
To break the mold,
Once
The dye is cast.

So hard
To know the future,
Til
It becomes the past.

Destiny

Am I
To be a relic
Of days
No longer here?

When my bones have turned to dust
And I am long forgotten,
Will there be another
Who feels the way I do?

Who has the inner vision
To see the world I see
And the voice of reason,
To alter destiny—

To stop
The self-destruction
Of man,
The earth, and sea?

Forever Searching

The pangs of hunger grow;
Still, I cannot eat.
My body, weak and weary;
Yet, I cannot sleep.

Filled with stress,
And overwrought,
I search for answers,
But all for naught!

Empty Love

When you love only money,
Your life is for naught.
For when you are dead,
The money you had,
Is just as quickly lost!

The Speaker

The tone
Denotes the kindness
In
The speaker's heart.

Carefully
Chosen words
Expose
The speaker's mind.

Sincerity
Of smile
Conveys
An earnest message.

So,
Listen very carefully
To what
The speaker says!

Less than Human

I speak,
Yet no one listens.
I hurt,
Yet no one cares.

I bleed
When I am cut.
Yet,
No one tends my wound.

I suffer
Alone in silence.
I am treated
As less than human.

I Remember Linda

I had a dream about Linda.
I remembered the fun we had.

The days filled with laughter,
The nights of sweet caress.

The walks along the beach.
The dancing cheek to cheek.

I had a dream about Linda.
I remembered a past so sweet.

Am I So Blind

Am I so blind
I cannot see
The truth
When it sits in front of me?

Am I so bound
By invisible chains
There is no way
For me to get free?

Am I
So afraid of change
I will not
Take a chance?

The Hunter

In the tropical jungle
The lion stalks his prey.
In the concrete jungle,
Man does the stalking
Much the same way.
Silently he creeps,
Hidden by the dark
Until a careless stranger
Ventures near his den
Where darkness hides the hunter,
Waiting his chance to strike.
The difference is the motive—
Man needs to conquer,
The lion needs to eat.

Cloud of Sadness

Veiled in a cloud of sadness,
Hidden from the light of joy,
I carry my burden of sorrow
Til happiness returns once more.

For just as day
Will follow night,
Time helps heal
A wounded soul.

Spirit of the Game

In the spirit of the game,
I live my life without refrain.
I sample the sweet, as well as the sour.
I live for the moment, not just the hour.

I endure the greatest pain,
That I may know the greatest joy.
The excitement of the journey
Enhances my arrival.

And when my life has ended,
And alive I am no more,
I will have died surely knowing
My life was pleasure-filled.

Demon in the Mist

At night I fight the shadows.
The daylight finds me hiding
From a world
I've come to fear.

The needle
Stirs my blood.
It brings me
Back to life.

Tonight
I will fight
A battle
I cannot win.

The day
Will find me hiding,
From
The "Demon in the Mist"!

Wings of Death

Floating on the surface,
Feet above the ground,
Inhaling dust of angels,
Smoking devil's weed.

Drinking Satan's poison
In the evening of the day.
Shadows of the future
Cause the light to dim.

Midnight Rendezvous

Waiting patiently
By the water's edge.
A midnight rendezvous
With a lover begins secretly.

Oh, sweet joy,
Hidden from the light.
Oh, sweet love,
Hidden by the night.

Hobo

Patiently waits the hobo
Beside the railroad track
For the coming train
He says will take him back

To his home
Of long ago.
In truth, he knows
He will not go.

Instead, another boxcar,
To another town.
Always the wanderer,
Until his life is done.

If You Can Say

If you can say, "I'm satisfied"
With the life that you have had.
If you can say, "No regrets,"
With life complete, when you are finally dead.

If you can rest, quite assured,
That you have done all you could
To leave this world a better place
Because you did pass through.

If you have reached your greatest heights
And become all that you could be,
Then your purpose here on earth
Has been quite fulfilled.

If Teardrops Were Wine

If
Teardrops were wine,
My glass
Would overflow.

The sorrow
That you gave me,
You
Will never know.

The
Lonely hours spent,
Trying
To forget,
Were all spent in vain
Because I still can feel the pain.

Words of Wisdom

Words of wisdom
Softly spoke
To a child
Just awoke,
Do so much
To confirm
That his world
Is full of love!

Cloud Beneath the Sun

The light is bright around me—
Yet still the shadow grows—
Veiling me in darkness,
Depriving me of light.

How can I find my way,
If I cannot see the path.
Will I remain forever lost
In a cloud beneath the sun?

Passion, Forever Gone

The wind is blowing through
Windows that will not close.
Alone and icy cold,
The doorway to my heart
May open never more.
The flames in the fireplace
Have flickered now and died.
The fire flowing through my veins
Is now a frozen pond.
And passion that I felt,
Is now forever gone.

A Tiny Hand

All alone, in the street
Stands a little boy.
Clothes worn and tattered,
Sadness in his eyes.

A tiny hand reaching out,
Hoping for a coin,
To ease once more the hunger
For another day.

Television

Sitting.
Staring.
Unknown faces
On television.

My mind wanders.
I see a vision,
But it's only
Television.

A Silent Peace

Cold sand
Between my toes.

Deserted beach,
A gentle rain.

A quiet stroll
To clear my brain.

A silent peace
Without a crowd.

Progress

Where once a mighty forest stood,
Concrete buildings now protrude.

No longer is the landscape green,
Gold, orange, purple and brown.

Now it is the grey
Of a growing town.

My Shanty Home

The wind blows icy cold
Outside my shanty home.

The leaky roof allows
The rain to penetrate.

The chill creeps inside
Through walls — paper thin.
But soon the rain will stop;
The wind will cease to blow.

The sun will shine again,
And warm my very soul.

Why Not Man?

To the will
Of the wind,
The strongest tree
Will surely bend.

Why then,
Does man not know
How to bend
Before he breaks?

When I Awake

Every morning
When I awake,
I thank the sun
  For rising.

And every evening
When work is done,
I am grateful I can see
The golden sun setting.

Happy Feet

Happy feet
Are walking
Down
The garden path.

Blooming flowers
Are smiling
At the early
Morning sun.

A Better You

Seek to find
Your needs in true.

And you will find
A better you!

How Can I Replace You?

How can I fill a void
As big as all outdoors?
How can I replace
Precious moments of the past?
Where can I find a love
As warm and as true?
The answer,
Quite simply is this:
When you left this world
For another,
You left behind
A lonely soul.
Your smile—
Unforgettable.
Your laugh—
Irreplaceable.
Your understanding—
Unbelievable.
Your compassion—
Immeasurable.
How can I replace you?
I cannot.

Lonely Streets

At night I walk
The lonely streets,
Cold
And all alone.

Looking for
A place of safety.
For a night,
To call my home.

Looking For the Light

I
Walked into darkness,
Looking
For the light.

I
Went to places strange,
To
Find a friendly face.

I looked
Toward the future,
Remembering
The past.

I looked
For hidden answers,
To questions
Never asked.

I looked
At my father,
To understand
My son.

I looked
At my brother,
To meet
My fellow man.

Searching

Searching for the future,
Hiding from the past.
Living in a present
I know can never last.

Santa

A jolly,
Gentle man,
With belly fat
And beard of white.

With
Warm heart
And
Kindly smile.

To every child,
Each year he brings
Toys, candy,
And other things.

A Moment of Inspiration

A moment
Of inspiration—
And like water,
Words did flow.

To fall
On empty pages—
And like magic,
Fill the scroll.

Recording
All of history
And events
Since time began.

To share the knowledge
Of the ages
With the children
Of mankind.

A Day for Mom

Mother's Day
Comes once a year.
The smallest gift
Will bring a tear
To a loving mother,
Year after year.

Do
Something special,
For your mom
On Mother's Day!

Memorial Day

A day to remember
The soldiers of peace
With a flower
Or a wreath.

A word of praise,
A tear of sadness
For the men
And the women.

They
Freely gave their lives
And paid
The price for freedom.

Is It Not

A rose,
Until it blooms,
Is but a plant.
Is it not?

And a lie
Is but a tale.
Until,
It is caught!

Americans

Adventurous.
Merciful, yet strong.
Earnest, efficient,
Resourceful.
Independent,
Courageous, proud.
America, forever free!

Peace

Peace and prosperity,
Everyone's dream—
Almost.
Care for your neighbor,
Everyone wins!

Before You Speak

When the thought
Does strike you
That something
Must be said,

Think
About the words
That will come
Out of your head!

Friend

If you find
Your friend in need,
Do not stand by
And watch him bleed.

If he falls
And needs a hand,
Take the time
To help him stand!

Some day you
May take a fall.
Then your friend
Will heed the call!

A moment lost in time
Will never come again.

Metal Monster

Swiftly
Go the metal monsters
Down
The concrete trail.

Always
In a hurry
To reach
Their destiny.

Throwing caution
To the wind,
They move
So carelessly.

Leaving death
And destruction
At every stop
They make.

Be cautious
As you travel,
Or your life
They may take!

Until

I have seen your soul.
I have read your heart.
I have loved you
From the very start.

What will be our future,
This, I do not know.
Except, that I shall love you
Until my dying day!

Reality

My perception of realty
Changes day by day.
That which once was right,
Now appears to be wrong.

The answer to the question,
Yesterday was yes.
But with an altered attitude,
Today it must be no.

Old, but Not Dead

I am getting old,
But I am not dead.
I can still laugh.
I can still cry.

Yet you try
To ignore me.
Please,
Tell me why?

Forever Today

There is no future.
There is no past.

The past—
Only memories.

The future—
Only dreams.

Only today
Is forever here.

George Washington

Our first president
Was not afraid to fight
For what he knew
Was right.

Through many cold
And bitter nights,
He led the long
And bloody fight.

With independence
Finally won,
He became
Our favorite son!

Blink of an Eye

In the blink of an eye
We are born.
In the blink of an eye
We die.

In cosmic
Time,
That
Is all we have.

A decision made in haste,
Can turn
The promised land,
Into
A burning waste.

The chance
To save tomorrow
Is such
A fleeting one.

Think long,
Think hard,
Before you take
The step of no return!

Life's Muddy Puddle

The puddle of life
Is muddy.
My future
Looks very dim.

My chances
Of being wealthy
Appear
To be very slim.

Investor's Dream

A field of gold,
A bed of green,
A river of ice—
That's my dream!

Tycoon's Prayer

As I lay me
Down to rest,
I pray the bank
Will line my vest

With silver
And with gold.
And do it before
I grow too old.

Crime

A bullet
Broke the silence
Of a peaceful
Summer night.

It stopped the
Would-be robber
In his
Tracks.

The robber
Took the hit,
And then
He quickly fell.

One shot
Was all it took
To send him
Straight to hell!